How to Make Money in Your Spare Time

By 637126

(Note: Author's Pen Name)

Table of Contents

Disclaimer: The information within this book is strictly intended for entertainment purposes. In no way does the author, publishing house, or any affiliate thereof condone or encourage the use of this information in any way that is against the law. Do not attempt any of the things found inside, and if you choose to do so, you are 100% liable for the subsequent repercussions.

PREFACE

Chances are, you have picked up this book because you have fallen on hard times. Most of us have. There is a reason why the 1% is called the 1%. It is because they are ballsy enough to take what they want, while the other 99% sit idly by, following policies, rules, and LAWS.

Let's get real, what the hell does any CEO know about the services, or products they offer? The answer? THEY DON'T! What they *do* know how to do is hustle. A lot of successful men, be it industry or politics, use unethical tactics to gain. The only difference between a criminal and a CEO is a matter of paperwork. In this book, you will learn how to be successful in your own way, yet in line with any successful businessman.

Keep in mind, however, that if you choose to be successful at any of this, you have to throw out any reserve, or ethics that you may have. That's right, forget about having empathy, forget about playing fair, and forget about keeping promises. That is exactly what that CEO does, and look at his paycheck!

Now, if you have decided to go on, congratulations, you are about to embark on an exciting and rewarding career that can be very lucrative for you. If you do things right, and if you are careful, you will come to realize that CRIME *DOES* PAY...

The following information contains a graded scale indicating the level of difficulty of each section. The scale rates as 1-5, 1 being the easiest and 5 being the hardest.

Additional ratings may be indicated by skillset recommended, in addition to the difficulty scale. More importantly, the information will also contain average prison sentences for the crimes discussed herein.

Chapter One:

EXTORTION

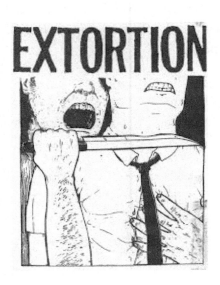

Difficulty Level: 2

Average Prison Sentence: 7 years

Skillset Required: Intimidating, Domineering, Charismatic

Let's just get right into something heavy, shall we? Merriam Webster defines extortion as *"the crime of getting money from someone by the use of force or threats"*. This is particularly effective if the extortionist is an authority figure. Think about it, all those tickets you got for speeding, the officer essentially said, "Pay the government X amount of money, or face a jail sentence". That's right, the government is the greatest extortionist, by using their authority and threatening something awful against you. And you

6

will pay every time. So how sweet would it be if you could do the same thing?

This is a favorite of "La Cosa Nostra" (the Italian Mob). For generations, oppressed Italian immigrants ran extortion rackets because the police refused to help them when something bad happened. So Mafiosi, or "men of honor", would offer that protection in return for monetary reimbursement.

Charles "Lucky" Luciano cr. 1936

Now, it's become more of a long-term robbery than anything else. Here's how you can get your beak wet in the extortion game:

Step 1. Pick a Mark: In order to extort someone, you have to make sure they won't go to the police. So many people get busted because their mark would rather hang on to their money than to give it willingly to the extortionist. So, you can avoid this by two things:

1. Make sure they are a "dirty" mark
2. Scare them bad enough they will stay quiet

A "dirty" mark is someone who has something to lose by going to the police. Either they are already doing something illegal and would not want to risk getting caught, or they have a public image they do not wish to tarnish. This is also a form of blackmailing, which we'll get into later.

Or, you could scare them bad enough by threatening to kill their pets, spouse, or children. You really want to hit them where it hurts, but remember, there is NO ROOM for empathy in this game. If you think you will feel bad later for threatening a child, then do not do it.

Step 2. Look Powerful: Now, once you have picked your mark, approach them with tenacity. Be suave in your movements, this shows that you are powerful and unafraid. Speak clearly, and smile. You do not want to alert the mark of your intentions right away, mainly because of the psychology involved, but also because you want to have plausible deniability later if you are arrested (we will discuss arrest in chapter eleven).

Step 3. Make Your Proposal: Be a little vague at first, such as, "Nice place you got here… it'd be a shame if something bad were to happen to it." And then stare unflinchingly into their eyes, smiling. Let them ponder what you just said for a minute. Then hit them with the, "pay me X amount a week, and I'll make sure nothing bad happens" bit. Now, if you decide to extort, remember that you HAVE TO FOLLOW THROUGH. Do not be a pussy now, you already committed the crime by saying what you said. If they do not pay, you have to follow through, i.e. burn the place down, or whatever gets you off.

Step 4. Commit: COMMIT. COMMIT. COMMIT. If you do not commit, they won't respect you, and if they do not respect you, they will go to the police.

If they do not pay you, your hand is forced, and you must do what you warned them about. (For blackmail, release the "dirt" or secret info you have on them, and enjoy the show.)

If they do pay you, you must collect from them, on a TIGHT SCHEDULE. DO NOT let them slack off on amounts, or deadlines.

BONUS: If they do slack off on paying the full amount, at least you know they are willing to pay in the first place. Make sure you do not do anything to them that will cause them to *not* be able to pay (burn down their establishment, kill them, disable them, etc.), just tack on the difference and charge them interest. When they rack up a debt to you, they will be forced to do whatever you want them to!

Let's review:

Step 1. Pick Your Mark

Make sure they're extort-able.

Step 2. Look Powerful

Weasels are not intimidating, but nobody fucks with a lion.

Step 3. Make Your Proposal

You want to get the point across in the most subtle way.

Step 4. Commit

Don't back down now.

If you are lucky, you will be able to make an income just by going to establishments, or people's houses once a week. Worked wonders for La Cosa Nostra.

Chapter Two:

DRUGS

Difficulty Level: 2

Average Prison Sentence: 2 Years

Skillset Required: Friendly, Sociable, Basic Math Skills

It is particularly ridiculous that we live in a society that gets to decide what we put in our bodies. How would you like it if I told you, "You can no longer drink coffee, and if you do, I'll have you thrown in jail"? I know drugs are not coffee, but that does not mean me or anyone else can tell you what you can or cannot consume. It is *your* fucking body.

With that said, there are two things you have to realize. First, people love drugs. They sell themselves! Second, as long as they are illegal, they will always be expensive. In a lot of cases, most people will pay for drugs before they pay their energy bills. But what drugs should you choose to sell?

"All I ever did was supply a demand that was pretty popular."

Al Capone on his bootlegging business

Step 1. Pick a Drug: Marijuana is great for those who do not want a dirty conscience. Most people who smoke weed are just regular people, hell I bet *you* smoke weed.

Cocaine is definitely expensive and not as bad as other drugs, but people still lose their heads over coke... literally. Most users are wealthy and therefore are more likely to pay higher prices.

Meth is always popular, but your risk of getting robbed is significantly higher and people will be coming to your place all hours of the night. You will have to consult the local market too, to see what is popular in your area. No point in having a bunch of illegal drugs when they won't even sell. Another reason to check your market is because of the Mexican drug cartels. These people play for keeps and if you "step on toes", they'll be inclined to chops *yours* off. Consider your options.

Drug Cartel beheading

Step 2. Buy in Bulk: This one is pretty obvious; buy in large amounts. Just like any retailer, if you buy in bulk from your wholesaler, you will get a discount.

You are also going to want to have a couple of different suppliers. When one dries up, you will need another to supply you.

11

The last place you want to be is out of drugs when your customers come calling.

Do NOT hassle your suppliers, do not let them screw you over, but do not hassle them either. When you irritate a supplier, they can "tax" you which means you end up paying a higher price than other people.

Step 3. Retain Your Customers: The drug business is a very word-of-mouth business. Everyone "knows a guy". Be the guy they know. Make sure you do not ever screw them over when you weigh out your sacks. You want the repeat business, and no one goes to a guy who screws them over. In fact, give a little bit extra in your sacks.

Do things that make them think you are one hell of a guy. Offer a little for free every once in a while. Samples are a great way to get them hooked, and coming back for more (with money). When they get something for free, they feel appreciated and give you more business.

Step 4. The Front: Eventually, you will come across someone who shows a propensity to sell. They may approach you and ask if they can sell with you. If you trust them, at least a little, give them some on a "front" (free upfront).

They take the stuff you front them, sell it off, and bring you back the money for a small take. Try to front to as many people as you can, that way you do not actually do any of the dealing. They do all the dealing for you, and you get to collect the paycheck.

WARNING: Working on fronts is dangerous, but necessary to become successful. If for some reason, the person you front refuses to pay, or cannot pay, you do what you have to. Refer to the chapter on extortion for this part.

Step 5. Incorporate: This is where you want to be. This is the most powerful position in a drug ring. You become the supplier, growing or manufacturing your own product, and then selling it off to distributors.

These distributors should be your partners. A tight network of people you trust, at least for the most part because YOU CAN NEVER TRUST ANYONE. Seriously, someone is going to screw you over, and it is probably going to be the person you trust most.

Give these distributors product on a front, and they come back with the price you ask. Their take is whatever they marked it up for. Let's say you supply them with a pound of marijuana on the notion that they will return to you with $2,000 (for instructive

purposes only). They would go and sell off ounces (there's 16 in that pound) for $200 an ounce. This nets a total of $3,200 tax free, to which their take would be $1,200 after bringing you the $2,000 you asked for in the first place.

Treat them well, because when the DEA comes knocking (and they will), you will want your distributors to be as loyal to you as possible.

Let's review:

Step 1. Pick a Drug

Make sure the market is not flooded and it sells well in your area.

Step 2. Buy in Bulk

The more you buy, the cheaper it is.

Step 3. Retain Your Customers

Treat them how you want to be treated.

Step 4. The Front

The more people who owe you, the better.

Step 5. Incorporate

Build a team of people you can somewhat trust.

It is a tough industry with a lot of violence. It is also cause for a hefty prison sentence, but you're a tough guy, right?

Chapter Three:

Racketeering

Difficulty Level: 4

Average Prison Sentence: 5 Years

Skillset Required: Business Skills, Algebra, Charismatic, Sales

Another La Cosa Nostra favorite, and this is as good as it gets for long-term goals. Racketeering, as it is commonly understood, has always coexisted with business. In the United States, the term racketeer was synonymous with members of organized-crime operations.

Congress passed RICO (Racketeer Influenced and Corruption Organizations 18 U.S.C.A. § 1961 et seq. [1970]) as part of the Organized Crime Control Act of 1970. Organized crime in the United States had been increasing ever since the Twenty-First Amendment's Prohibition of alcohol was repealed in 1933. Crime groups and families that had been bootlegging moved on to other moneymaking crimes by controlling legitimate businesses and by using some of them as fronts for criminal activity. Over the years, Congress had enacted several statutes authorizing increased punishment for typical organized-crime activities such as illicit gambling rings, loan sharking, transportation of stolen goods, and Extortion. However, it had not passed legislation that specifically punishes the very act of committing organized crime.

You have to be crafty to come up with a racket. Gambling is a good one. So for now, we will use gambling as an example but by all means, substitute what you wish in its place.

Step 1. Pick a Group: Unlike drugs, instead of picking product first, you want to pick a group of people. These people will be seeing a lot of each other, so make sure they get along. This group you pick will be playing poker against each other under your watch.

Make sure these guys have a lot of money, and they won't freak out or do something rash if they lose it. Just in case, make sure they have something nice to offer for collateral if you ever need to collect (just don't let them know you're targeting it).

Step 2. Set it up: Now that you have your group, you will need a place. Hotel suites make for perfect mini casinos. You could use other places to host your game, such as a restaurant after hours, or a home. You will need to use your imagination.

After you get the place settled, you will need to offer poker supplies, such as chips, and cards. Make sure you use more than one deck so a fresh shuffled deck is always ready to go. Card games can go all night, so in order to speed things up, use more than one deck. You can also speed the game up by using a computer program that automatically increases the antes, or the blinds if you are playing Texas Hold 'Em. These programs are free online, should you choose to use them.

Other supplies you will need are cigars, cigarettes, alcohol, and food and water. Have young, and attractive girls there to serve your players so they will be more inclined to gamble big.

Along with your servers, you will need protection in case things get out of control, and they will. Anytime someone loses their ass in a bet you can be sure they will do anything to get it back, so have some muscle around.

Now, as far as the actual game goes, you do not need to do anything; just let them play. They will know how to deal, how to bet, etc. What you do want to do however, is make sure they understand that out of every pot (betting pool), you "rake" 10 points. So out of every round, you get 10% from the winnings. Just take the chips out of the pot, and at the end of the night when everyone cashes out, there will be an amount of cash left over that corresponds to the chips you raked. Which brings us to banking.

You will be the bank, so when a player gives you his cash, you give him chips. Then, you guard that money with your life, and your hired muscle should help. Keep it locked away with whoever you decide to run the computer program you logged onto.

Step 3. Continue, but Switch it up: Keep your gambling racket going. This is a nice way to generate cash flow. Encourage your players to bring other high rollers (just make sure they're not wired for sound).

You will want to change the locations up every once in a while, just in case the feds are onto you. Sometimes, leave the game to your partner's charge if you have one. That way, no one knows who really runs the operation.

BONUS: Some guys are just itching to get their lost monies back, so if you so choose, you can loan them money to gamble with. When this happens, it is because the player has lost all his money, and he is desperate for a return. This means you can charge him a ridiculous interest rate on your loan, and he will oblige! This is the type of guy you want to have collateral. Let's say he owns a car dealership... if he slips up, you can have any car you want, all on his dime! Not to mention being partner of a car dealership has its other advantages, such as a way to launder all your money, which we will discuss in chapter ten.

Review:

Step 1. Pick a Group

The more money they have, the better your paycheck.

Step 2. Set it up

Take your time with this, foundation is everything.

Step 3. Continue, but Switch it up

The more confusion about the operation, the better. Do not let them get too close to your inner circle.

Chapter Four:

Bootlegging or Smuggling

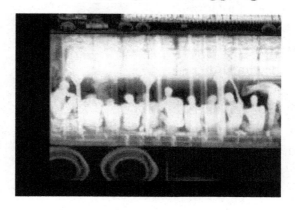

Difficulty Level: 2

Average Prison Sentence: 5 Years

Skillset Required: Technical Skills, Basic Math, Sales

Bootlegging became popular during prohibition, where alcohol was banned in the U.S. People like to drink, so naturally, there became a black market for the stuff. Bootlegging actually means transferring and selling a product without permission, or illegally. Smuggling is practically the same thing, but it can be a legal product. What makes smuggling illegal is not paying proper licenses or taxes on the movement of the product.

If you think about it, it is almost as if the government WANTS you to bootleg or smuggle products. Why else would they charge such an outrageous tax? Or business permits and licensing? They are practically begging for it, so I say you just give them what they want. Others have done it, and made a decent living at it.

Al Capone, for example, was a very successful bootlegger. He ran operations in Chicago and even had a chair on the commission of the Five Families in New York. His campaign involved bootlegging alcohol into the city, where it was sold at "speakeasies" or secret bars. Bootlegging and smuggling can be very profitable, but you have to know the risk and rewards. Check your local laws to see how hefty a penalty can be.

Alphonse Capone

Step 1. Acquire a Product: Al Capone did it with alcohol. You can still do it, since it is very difficult to acquire a liquor license. But since it *is* legal, you will have to pick something else, like bootleg DVDs if you want to make a bigger profit. A lot of people do it, but if your product is of decent quality, you can make a killing!

Some people smuggle cigarettes. While cigarettes are not illegal, the selling of them can be if you do not pay proper taxes on them. New York, for example, has the highest tax rate on cigarettes. Some people pay up to $14 a pack! There was once an operation where two brothers bought cigarettes in Virginia (where the tax is incredibly low), and resold them in New York for lower prices. Without paying the New York tax, of course. This is smuggling, and it made these brothers rich until they got caught.

Step 2. Establish a Trade Route: You will need to have a way to sell your product. At this point, you should already know roughly how to do this. If it is bootleg DVDs, sell them in front of other video stores if you are sure you will not be hassled by police. Find a place your customers shop.

For cigarettes, try your hand in high taxed areas like New York, or even California. If you are smart, you will help to encourage bills proposed to congress for increasing taxes on your product.

If you are doing the transporting yourself, be advised, OBEY ALL TRAFFIC LAWS. Do not be an idiot, and speed, or roll through stop signs, or forget to use your signals. That being said, check all your lights to make sure none are burned out. The last thing you want is a cop getting suspicious of you because you cannot hold your cool with a metric ton of ripped off DVDs in your trunk, all because he stopped you for a burned out tail light.

Keep in mind, if a cop wants to search your car, he will. He does NOT need your permission. You can argue your rights, saying he needs a warrant, but he will just get a drug dog out to your car, and cause a false positive. Dogs are easy to trick into clawing at something, or to get roused. This creates the "reasonable suspicion" so he can legally search your car.

If you see signs that say "CHECKPOINT AHEAD", do NOT try to dodge it. By the time you see the sign, it is already too late. It is better to chance it, and keep your cool. If the sign says "DRUG CHEKPOINT AHEAD", ignore it completely. The police cannot legally operate a  "drug checkpoint" so you are in the clear.

Step 3. Reward Your Regular Buyers: If you have successfully acquired a regular buyer, do everything in your power to encourage their business further.

Make Money in Your Spare Time

If you chose to smuggle tax free smokes, and your buyer runs a convenient store where he sells your smuggled cigarettes, give him a free carton every once in a while. Give him a personal bottle of champagne, or cigars or something. Take him out to a nice meal to express your gratitude. Let's face it, the guy is risking his business in support of yours, so return the favor!

In review:

Step 1. Acquire a Product

It can literally be anything, but illegal things make more money.

Step 2. Establish a Trade Route

Be persuasive, be a salesman.

Step 3. Reward Your Regular Buyers

Legitimate businesses often have rewards programs, so you should offer rewards, too.

Chapter Five:
Theft/Robbery

Difficulty Level: 3

Average Prison Sentence: 5 years

Skillset Required: Intimidating, Detail Oriented, Focused

Now, thieves are typically despised people. However, you will do what you must in order to survive and if that involves stealing, then so be it. Theft has been around since mankind has been around. It has been a productive way for people to make ends meet for centuries.

You know the cartoon with the infamous "street rat" who stole bread from the market with his pet monkey? He was doing it to survive. Some people, however, do it for profit. Some will steal something that they want, or something that sells well, which is called "fencing" and we will discuss it in the next chapter. Some people also steal money, and that is it. Decide what it is you want to steal, and how you want to earn your money from it.

Robbery can be a traumatizing event, particularly for the individual you are robbing, but it is also traumatizing for the robber. When you choose to rob, rather than using stealth to take what you want, you are using force. This obviously creates a thought pattern in your head which generates panic, paranoia, and even a "fog of war". Fog of war is typically a great confusion that occurs on the battlefield. Well, when you commit a robbery, you are in a battlefield. Think wisely in choosing your method.

Step 1. Choose a Target: This can either be a person, or a place, or a thing. Places are easier to steal from than people, though. If you want to try and pick pocket someone, make sure you are skillful at it, it goes without saying.

If you choose a place, make sure there are no cameras, or at least the cameras will not be able to see who you are. Remember, there are cameras outside, too, even at other locations so it is suggested that you do not drive *your* car there. In fact, walking could be your best bet, unless you take the plates off, or steal a car for the job.

As far as robbery goes, let's be honest; with the stricter gun laws America has been imposing on herself, targets are becoming more readily available to robbers. Although, you can never really tell who has a gun, you can increase your chances by profiling your target.

We all profile, every single one of us. It is the sad truth of society, but that is how our species survives. You know better than to approach a strange individual in a dark alley, and that is profiling.

ALL IN FAVOR OF "GUN CONTROL" RAISE YOUR RIGHT HAND

Adolph Hitler Disarmed

Europe

Make sure your target looks weaker than you. While they may not be, chances are that they won't put up a fight. Clean cut, middle-aged men make good targets. Middle-aged because they probably have children, and will not risk orphaning those kids over a handful of cash. Look to see what they drive. If it is an older car, that does not appear to be expensive, chances are that your target is a broke loser.

Sometimes, you could actually target OTHER ROBBERS! Go to notorious areas, armed of course, and watch the place like a vigilante. As soon as you see a robbery take place, attack the robber. Be careful because at this point, the robber will kill you if he has to so you may have to open fire first. Then, take what he took. You can either take off or return it to the rightful owner. They will be so appreciative of you, often times they will offer you a reward for your heroism. Only you and I know what you were really doing out there…

Step 2. Get as Much as You Can: You do not want to spend too much time at the scene, but you want to make sure it is at least worth your troubles. Stealing $20 would not be worth it if you got caught. This is why you have to get what you can, and spend absolutely no more than five minutes at the scene. Anything after five minutes, the victim will begin to think of ways out or ways to get back at you. Five minutes and NO MORE.

If you choose to do it robbery style, the scarier the better. Wear a mask, and dark clothes. Change your voice to sound more intimidating. Use a big gun, like a shotgun because it is scary as hell. People know that it is harder to dodge a shotgun blast than a handgun bullet. Especially if the barrel is sawn shorter so that the spread of the cartridge is much greater.

Be loud, boisterous, cocky, and threatening. The last thing anyone wants to do is turn a robbery into a murder. The more they believe you will end them if they do not pay, the better your chances of getting away with cash in hand.

After you make your point and tell them what you want, make sure you check everywhere money is likely to be kept. If it is a store, check all tills, drop boxes, and the store safe located most often in the office. Also, grab expensive items that you have seen sell quickly before. You can make a decent profit fencing those items later. Keep that in mind for the next chapter.

Step 3. Hook the Victims Up: If you are robbing a store for example, give the employees or any other shoppers a take of the money or product you steal. This not only makes you seem like a Robin Hood with the locals but it really confuses the people who are about to call the cops on you. It not only buys you a few seconds, but later, when they are interrogated by the police, their memories become clouded by images of you giving them free crap.

Avoid hurting anyone if you can. That way, if you are ever caught, your penalties won't be as harsh.

Step 4. Lay Low: Now, your natural instinct will be to boast or brag about your recent exploits. DO NOT do this! Again, it goes without saying. Resist the urge to look really cool in front of your friends, your co-workers, or even your family. The more people who know, the greater your chances of getting caught.

Now, you will have a good sized chunk of change which you will want to spend right away, or you stole it because you need it right away, but don't spend it just yet! Wait until everything dies down, or the heat is off. If people see you spending a lot of money suddenly, it will look suspicious.

If it is product that you stole, leave it in your closet for a while. At the very least 3 months. If someone's favorite watch goes missing they will immediately go hunting for it, checking every watch they see because they feel violated and crave justice. If you happen to have it on while the owner is gunning for it, you are just asking for problems.

If for some reason your face was seen, or you could be placed at the scene of the crime, change your looks the best way you can. Grow a beard, shave a beard, dye hair (don't do a bad job, it makes it look obvious), change tattoos, whatever!

Time for the review

Step 1. Choose a Target

The easier, the better. You don't want a lot of obstacles in this industry.

Step 2. Get as Much as You Can

You only have about five minutes, so know where to look.

Step 3. Hook the Victims Up

It will help to cloud a witness's memory.

Step 4. Lay Low

Depending on how much you got, and what you did to get it, you could be a felon.

If you are good at paying attention to details, this one could be your bread and butter. Stay focused on the prize and just a tip; do not become too greedy.

Chapter Six:

Fencing

Difficulty Level: 1

Average Prison Sentence: 1 Year (First Offense)

Skillset Required: Willpower, Sales, Hustling Skills, Business Mindset

Fencing is a great way to make huge profit margins. The definition of fencing is knowingly buying stolen goods at a low price, to resale for a higher price later on. Thieves will gladly sell you something stolen for almost nothing just so they can lose the heat.

John Gotti was known to fence women's clothing, so much so that he made most of his fortune from it. In Charles Dickenson's 19th century story, *Oliver Twist*, the character "Fagin" recruits homeless boys to pickpocket victims so that he could later sell the stolen items. Fencing is an old and timeless business but with serial numbers on almost everything now, you have to be very cautious.

Step 1. Purchase the Stolen Goods: Thieves will sell stolen property for literally pennies on the dollar. You could pay them so low, or not even pay them at all. You could just threaten telling the police unless they give you some stuff for free. The hard part is *finding* the supplier. Meth addicts are usually a solid choice because they need their fix so bad, they will actually steal items that you want them to, just for a hit of the magic powder!

WARNING: Meth heads are volatile and unpredictable, and they will turn on you quicker than you know. Watch your back too, because if they get arrested, they WILL rat you out.

Make sure you know the retail value of the item in question so that you do not pay retail prices. In addition to that knowledge, you must also know roughly what you could sell it for in the market. If you neglect this very important part, you will undoubtedly lose money and you're not about that.

Step 2. Lay Low: The heat is on for the stolen property, so just hold on to it for a while. Remember the minimum amount of time? Three months at least. If you purchased electronics or expensive tools, there will be identification markings.

Remove any identification or any serial numbers. If it is obvious that you removed the serial numbers, it will be more difficult to sell the product. This means your profits will be less, and you're not about that either.

Step 3. Sell in a Different Market: You can sell in the same town the stuff was stolen from if you choose to do so, but the chances of you getting caught increase. It is strongly suggested that you transport your goods to another town and sell it there.

It will be difficult to build a client base this way, so it is best to go to a town that you are either familiar with, or that you have friends and family in. This way you have an anchor or a branch, if you will, in the town you want to sell goods in.

NEVER SELL ONLINE! The person who was robbed has the internet, and believe me, they are looking for their stuff on there. Sure, you might get away with it a few times but eventually, YOU WILL GET CAUGHT. If you do get caught, depending on how much dollar value the items have and how much you earned on them will dictate your prison sentence. First time offenders usually get a year, which is not bad but even a day in lock-up is one day too many. Remember, the United States may be the land of the free but it is also the home of the most prisoners. Don't become a number.

Fencing is relatively easy once you get a supplier. The hardest part is finding one, but once you do, you can let your hustling skills do all the work in this fun, and rewarding career choice!

Let's review, shall we?

Step 1. Purchase Stolen Goods

Find yourself a meth addict hurting for a bump. They'll steal the whole Earth for you.

Step 2. Lay Low

The last thing you want is to be caught with a few thousand dollars' worth of stolen stuff.

Step 3. Sell in a Different Market

Don't "shit where you eat", they say.

Chapter Seven:

Contract Steering

Difficulty Level: 5

Average Prison Sentence: 4 Years

Skillset Required: Charismatic, Extraverted, Business Mindset, Hustling Skills

A personal favorite of any white collar criminal! Contract steering means you are ensuring that a preferred company is given a contract to do a job. You "steer" that contract to them.

Some people have done this when job hunting without even knowing it. When you apply for a job you are putting in a bid on it. You are saying to them, "I will be the best choice, the least expensive, and I will provide the most work". But then, when you get hired, you don't do much of anything you promised.

Some people steer contracts with blackmail. For example, if you wanted the landscaping contract for a few parks in your county, and you happen to know the county comptroller hangs out at the local strip club and his wife does not know, guess who just landed the contract?

Contract steering is difficult to pull off mainly because you have to know people in places a little higher than your own, but for instructional purposes, here is how you do it on a small scale.

Step 1. Pick a Company: You can do this with your own company if you have one, but the farther you associate your legitimate self to this, the better.

Let's say you choose a concrete company; "Joe's Cement". Make sure Joe is hurting for money because if he is, it will be that much easier to get him to willingly commit a felony.

Tell him you can make his money troubles go away and that you and you alone can get him a contract to build sidewalks for the new city development. All he has to do is give you a small cut from the contract.

Once he agrees, you better get to work immediately because the longer he has to wait for the money, the longer he has to think about the consequences of what he is doing. This may make him change his mind, so the quicker you get on it, the better.

Step 2. Schmooze the Politician Who Gives the Contracts: Politicians are stupid, and very easy to schmooze. They are all the same. They love to hear about themselves and how good of a leader they are. Play them like a fiddle but do not overdo it; any self-respecting schmoozer knows when they are being fed bull.

Step 3. Make Him an Offer He Can't Refuse: In order for them to hand over the contract to "Joe's Cement", you will have to make sure it is worth it for him. No one wants to risk a decent career, especially politicians.

Let him know he will get a fat check made payable to him directly to use for whatever he wishes; charity, his political campaign, a new pool, whatever. Just make it a large percentage, otherwise there is no incentive for him. You cannot afford to be greedy on this part. Save that greed for the meth head you hired to fence.

If the politician in question does not want to be a part of this operation, make him want to be a part of it. If it is not money he wants, then threaten him. You can either use violence, or fear.

The politician is a public figure who cannot afford to look bad. You can invite him out to dinner for a business meeting or you can pay someone off in his office, but find a way to get him to pass out. One good way is to slip him a Xanax. Mixed with alcohol, the effects are similar to Rohypnol (roofies). Once he is incapacitated, take photos of him with a few skanky girls you can pay off. Then blackmail him later.

Step 4. Remove Competition: If for some reason step 3 is unattainable, you must remove your competition. You may have to do this part regardless of political cooperation. This is because if you are audited, and the politician in question is audited, there is no question as to why you won the contract even though other companies offered lower prices. Government contracts ALWAYS go to the lowest bidder, and if you are *not* the lowest bidder, there will be a red flag.

You remove your competition by whatever means necessary. You have several options in doing so. You can murder them, destroy their equipment or buildings, or threaten them. You are only limited by your imagination.

Step 5. Follow Up: Once the contract is made, and "Joe's Cement" gets their money, pay them a visit for your cut. Be very friendly with the business owner because he will most likely want to do a venture like that again and you will be Johnny on the spot.

When you make your "partners" happy, they make you happy. It is as simple as that! Joe might even want to take you out to celebrate, which means free meals for you, and later he may want to discuss partnering up with you. That means you now have a storefront to launder money which we will discuss later.

This is the sneakiest way to make a lot of money. If you do it right, you will become richer than you could ever have expected but make sure you follow the steps.

In review:

Step 1. Pick a Company

You want them to *want* your help.

Step 2. Schmooze the Politician

If you don't make him a friend, he will be of no use.

Step 3. Make Him an Offer He Can't Refuse

DON'T be greedy. Make it worth his time, and he'll respect you in the long run.

Step 4. Remove Competition

Nobody wants competition anyways. That means you have no price control.

Step 5. Follow Up

Stay on good terms with everyone involved, that way you can do it again and again.

Chapter Eight:

Confidence Games

Difficulty Level: 4

Average Prison Sentence: 10 years (Big Cons)

Skillset Required: Charisma, Lying, Detail Oriented

A confidence game, or con, is when a person is tricked by the exploitation of characteristics of the human psyche such as greed or power. You must first win their trust on a confidence game, and this is where the name "confidence" stems from; GAIN THEIR CONFIDENCE.

There are two types of cons; the short con and the long con. Short cons are used for quick money, which means little sums of money. Long cons are cons that take a longer amount of time, but have much larger pay-offs. Ponzi schemes are notoriously lucrative long cons. Look at Bernie Madoff and all the money he conned! Short cons are much easier to pull off.

A short con is a trick a confidence man will pull in order to make a quick buck. An example of this is the Glim Dropper. It typically requires a one-eyed person, but use your imagination if you cannot acquire one. In the Glim Dropper, the one-eyed man goes inside a store, and pretends to lose his glass eye. After searching everywhere for it, he gives up and offers the storekeeper $1,000 reward for the non-existent glass eye. The next day, you go inside, and pretend to have found a glass eye. The storekeeper will be so excited that you found it and he will want you to give it to him. Get him to offer some money in exchange for it. He will probably give you no more $200, but that is a good amount. After all, he's going to get $1,000, right? You leave with money in hand, and he becomes the new owner of a $200 glass eye that no one actually lost in the first place.

Another way this can be done is with a "lost dog", or sentimental artifact. Other cons can be as simple as you want, such as running a fake raffle.

In a fake raffle, you have people purchase tickets at extremely cheap prices, yet have the winning prizes so rewarding that the victim cannot refuse buying a few tickets. A brand new video game system, or a laptop, or even a large amount of drugs.

When you have your "drawings" you plant a guy in the crowd. This plant is someone who will "win" the raffle drawing, but no one is keen to the fact that you and the plant had a prior arrangement that you would call off his ticket, he would act like he won, and you give him a few bucks instead of the prize. The best part is no one can prove you rigged it. All of your victims will have believed that your plant won the drawing fair and square.

Confidence games can be pretty easy, but you still have to put a lot of things together first and make sure they stay together. If you fail at any part of the con, you risk getting found out.

Step 1. Foundation Work: The preparations which are made before the scheme is put in motion, including the elaboration of the plan, the employment of assistants and coconspirators. Choose your con, and then begin the planning of it.

Step 2. Approach: The manner of getting in touch with the victim—often most elaborately and carefully prepared. It is very important you do not mess this up. Be at your utmost convincing.

Step 3. Build-up: Rousing and sustaining the interest of the victim, introducing the scheme to him, rousing his greed, showing him the chance of profit and filling him with so much anticipation and cupidity that his judgment is warped and his caution thrown away. Then he will be putty in your hands.

Step 4. Pay-off or Convincer: An actual or apparent paying of money by the conspirators to convince the victim and settle doubts by a cash demonstration. In the old banco game, the initial small bets which the victim was allowed to win were the pay-off. In stock swindles the fake dividends sent to stockholders to encourage larger investments are the pay-off. Make sure you use pay-offs to get the bigger bucks!

Step 5. The Hurrah: This is like the dénouement in a play and no con scheme is complete without it. It is a sudden crisis or unexpected development by which the sucker is pushed over the last doubt or obstacle and forced to act. Once the hurrah is sprung the victim is fully entrusting in you or there is no game.

When the one-eyed man desperately offered $1,000 reward for his glass eye, he sprung the hurrah. You can do the same in many different ways. If it is for stocks, you can claim that competition against the "company" have been bought out, or bankrupted. This will give the illusion of a monopoly controlled by your "company", which means controlled prices and higher dividends.

Step 6. The In-and-In: This is the point in a con game where you put some of your money into the deal with that of the victim; first, to remove the last doubt that may tarry in the gull's mind, and, second, to put the con man in control of the situation after the deal is completed, thus forestalling a squeal. Often the whole game is built up around this feature and just as often it does not figure at all.

If you plan everything out in the beginning, including a contingency plan, then you can stand to make a lot of money this way. Who knows, you may even make enough money to buy your own penthouse in New York.

Review time:

Step 1. Foundation Work

Take the time to plan properly. A house cannot stand without a solid foundation.

Step 2. Approach

The more convincing you are, the more money you can potentially make.

Step 3. Build Up

"Fake it 'til you make it" they say. Make the victim jealous of your success, and make him want it.

Step 4. Pay-off or Convincer

The better the pay-off, the more they'll spend on you.

Step 5. The Hurrah

Get rid of any doubt they may have, forcing them to act.

Step 6. The In-and-In

Invest yourself with the victim, giving yourself a stronghold over their trust.

Chapter Nine:

Cyber Scamming

Difficulty Level: 5

Average Prison Sentence: Varied

Skillset Required: Technical Skills, Detail Oriented, Computer Skills

I would not recommend cyber scamming for one reason, and one reason alone. YOU MUST BE A HACKER TO PULL THIS OFF. Otherwise, you risk getting caught because it is easy to track down IP addresses.

Depending on how you choose to do this one, it will require a lot of set up, so for ease, the examples will not be very grandiose. Besides, this is so you can make money in your *spare* time, not as a full time job.

The easiest way to do this is via social networks, or email. It is similar to a short con, but it is all via the internet. No interaction in person is required.

Step 1. Create a Phony Website: Create a website that mimics that of a popular banking institution. You must make it as convincing as possible, so you may wish to hire a professional for this one. This is very illegal, so make sure the web designer you hire is on the level.

On this site, you will require the victim to enter their confidential information, which you then steal and use to claim hundreds or thousands of dollars for yourself.

Step 2. Send Emails: Send emails to any possible configuration you can think of or find lists of random emails online. Make the email you send to them in HTML. There are site generators for the design on an HTML email, but they cost money. It is still cheaper than hiring someone else to do it. Another option is learning how to create HTML emails yourself, then you could save yourself the money it costs to hire someone or pay a site.

The email needs to be as convincing as possible so make sure you use similar styles by that of whatever banking institution your website is cloned from. Using logos, lingo, and even special offers at the bottom make it all the more convincing.

In the email, inform the victim of the urgent matter that their identity needs verification. Provide a link with them to click on to verify their identity. This link takes them to the phony website you created where the victim will fill in their information.

Step 3. Use Their Info: Use the information you have stolen to log in to their bank accounts, and wire money to yourself or a partner via Western Union. It is very hard to trace money that has been wired this way, and it is your best bet in not getting caught.

Other ways you can do this is online shopping, and use their bank account info to make purchases from online stores. Have the goods delivered to a P.O. Box, or another location that you can stakeout when the delivery arrives. Then, run out and snatch the package before the real tenant notices. This way, if the authorities do take notice, they arrest someone else and not you.

Step 4. Take Small Amounts: In order to buy yourself time to make a lot of money, take only small, relatively unnoticeable amounts of money from them. The larger the sum in question, the larger the red flag.

It is much better to steal $20 from 1,000 people every month than to steal $1,000 from 20 people one time.

If you have the skillset or resources for this one, it can be very lucrative. Keep in mind that if IP addresses are tracked, it can lead to trouble. Either be or hire a hacker, or use a public computer.

Let's Review what we've learned in this chapter:

Step 1. Create a Phony Website

Make it exactly like the real deal.

Step 2. Send Emails

Just spam everyone possible.

Step 3. Use Their Info

Hack in to every account they have.

Step 4. Take Small Amounts

Take little over a long period of time to avoid red flags.

Chapter Ten:

Money Laundering

Difficulty Level: 3

Average Prison Sentence: 4 years

Skillset Required: Technical Skills, Detail Oriented

Money laundering occurs when an individual "purifies" illegal money through a means of forgery. The illegal funds are typically funneled through a company to make it appear as if the money was obtained through legal transactions.

According to Page Pate, with the Pate Law Firm, "A person commits money laundering when he performs a financial transaction with knowledge that the property involved came from a particular illegal act. Money laundering also requires an intention to further the illegal act. It should be noted that a person need not actually succeed in completing an illegal transaction to be convicted. An attempted illegal transaction is enough."

44

So, let's say you have a ton of money you made with any one of the ways shown in this book. If you go around town buying super expensive things with cash and you do not have a job that pays wages to afford lavish things, what will people say? Do you think it is wise to flaunt loads of money when your day job is retail sales at a chain franchise?

So what's the point of having all that money and *not* being able to spend it? The good news is you *can* spend it, but only once it has been purified. The way to do it offers a means to quitting your day job, and working your hustle full time! It is money laundering in its finest form: *Setting up a front to launder the illegal money.*

Step 1. Create the Front: You can do this in many ways. What you want to obtain here is a legitimate business that can show records of legal and taxable transactions. Yes, it is sad that you must pay taxes on illegal money where you charged no tax in the first place, but hey, where do politicians get *their* money? Illegal money obtained by "collecting evidence" on the criminal who owns it, or laundered money funneled through legitimate means that will be taxed. What does this mean? Adjust your prices accordingly to account for the taxes you will be charged later, or risk losing it all anyways.

You can either move in on an established business via means of extortion, or bribery and corruption. Everyone has a price! Your other option is to set up your own business.

Setting up your own business is difficult, but not if you make the right moves. There are some dos and don'ts to this, and they are as follows:

Do: Apply for a business license

Do: Keep records

Do: Obey all laws

Do: Make sure it is a business that can almost run itself (you'll be busy doing other stuff)

Do: Hire employees that are permitted to work

Do: Hire a crooked accountant to launder the money

And

Don't: Deal with hazard waste (no need for EPA inspections)

Don't: Allow it to require you there constantly

Don't: Ignore local laws and zoning requirements

Don't: Forget to show up every once in a while

Now that your front is set up, you can move on to the next step.

Step 2. Forge Transactions: You can do this by ringing up items at the register, and stuffing the cash in there yourself, or by forging documents and invoices to reflect more transactions. These transactions of course are not really occurring, but now you have a way to explain where that extra $15,000 in cash came from...

To do it in the form of the latter, you will need to employ a very savvy and crooked accountant. Now, most accountants are a little crooked anyways, so in order to push them over the edge and to join the dark side with you, offer cash incentive. They will know how to explain your generous donations to the IRS later, don't worry.

Hire the accountant and have him or her do all the work for you. This way you can focus on obtaining more revenue, which of course keeps your account in business.

Step 3. Claim it as Taxable Income: If you look at your tax statements, you will notice a line dedicated to the claiming of illegal monies. An official statement from the IRS says, "Income from illegal activities, such as money from dealing illegal drugs, must be included in your income on Form 1040, line 21, or on Schedule C or Schedule C-EZ (Form 1040) if from your self-employment activity."

Not surprisingly, few criminals report this income. However, if you are tried and you did *not* claim your income, you can be charged with tax evasion. Al Capone is probably the most notable figure for this example. While the government could not arrest him for illegal activities, they *were* able to make an arrest for tax evasion. Pay your taxes!

This does not mean to claim the money as illegal money, rather, claim it as income from your front.

Step 4. Bank in Foreign Countries: The media often depicts the disgustingly rich having bank accounts in foreign countries, such as the Cayman Islands. This is because most rich people do bank out of country. One reason is because they, too, launder questionable money.

In a lot of foreign countries such as Switzerland or the Caymans, the banks have a strict privacy policy that will not allow US officials to investigate their customers. This is good for people like you needing to hide the loot. However, not all rich people are laundering money, but most *are* trying to avoid paying taxes.

In the US, you are taxed a ridiculous amount of money constantly. Allow me to paint a picture for you:

When you buy a house, the money you spend purchasing it is taxed. When the owner who sells you the home is paid, he pays a tax on *that*. Then, while you are living in the home, you must pay an additional property tax every single year. If you rent out a room, you must pay taxes on the rent. You must also pay taxes when you buy something with the rent money you've generated. And, if you decide to sell the home, you will pay taxes on the sale as well.

You see how crooked the government is? Do you see the extortion they've been committing and getting away with? You don't need to pay these crooks another dime. Instead, bank out of country. Whatever money you receive, or spend, do it via your foreign bank and forget about the taxes!

In retrospect:

Step 1. Create the Front

Make it completely legitimate, you don't want any investigations.

Step 2. Forge Transactions

Make the cash clean.

Step 3. Claim it as Taxable Income

The government doesn't care how you make your money, so long as you pay your tributes.

Step 4. Bank in Foreign Countries

Try to limit the taxation on yourself without fearing indictment.

Chapter Eleven:

What to do if You're Arrested

Most cops are cops because they were either bullies in high school, and they want to get paid to be a bully, or they *got* bullied in high school and they want their payback. Either way, you are likely to have a jerk as an arresting officer. Your best bet is to kiss his or her ass.

Let's say you are driving along and you have a kilo of cocaine in the trunk. If you are pulled over, it is not because he thinks you have a kilo of cocaine in your trunk (even though he could be suspicious of it because you fit the profile of a cocaine dealer. I recommend checking out "Never Get Busted Again" by Barry Cooper at nevergetbusted.com to learn more).

If you are pulled over though, it is likely because of some other reason; turn signal, tail light, illegal turn, speed, etc. When the officer approaches be very cordial and show respect. Do not be a hot head. If you get a ticket, accept it. It is the price you pay to avoid a prison sentence.

Now, if you are arrested by this officer and then they wish to search your car, immediately state the following:

"I do not give the police permission to search my vehicle."

Repeat it loudly to ensure the dash camera picks it up. Other than this, SAY NOTHING. Your Fifth Amendment Right protects you from saying anything incriminating, so clam up and wait for your lawyer.

Lawyers are expensive and they may require a retainer (payment to keep you on the books as a regular client to them). Any fee they charge is worth it. This way you do not accidentally screw yourself over by begging for mercy or whatever the cop offers you. They are LYING.

That's correct. Cops are people too, and people often lie. Most officers are promoted based on the amount of arrests they make. So while there are no quotas to fill, there are personal scores that are kept in order for an officer to further his or her career. This means they will do what they can to ensure you go away for a while. This is bad for business.

In your new career choice, you will undoubtedly have encounters with the law. Luckily for you, there are techniques you can use in order to deal with these encounters.

Step 1. Be Cordial: Like stated earlier, cops are people too. You can appeal to their good nature by being as nice, friendly, and cooperative as possible.

NEVER EVER RUN. Running admits guilt. If you look guilty, you *are* guilty and that will stick all the way through your trial. Besides, running from the police is embarrassing. DO NOT RUN.

If he asks you, "do you know why I pulled you over?" Do not respond with, "'Cause you want the 'D'." Just say something along the lines of "yes, sir/no, sir" etc.

Step 2. Don't Resist, but be Stern: Do not resist the police. This gets them agitated, and they have been known to demonstrate brutal acts of violence when provoked. Even though they are the police, they are just as corrupt as anyone else.

This does not mean to capitulate, you should be rather stern and unyielding still. Be sure to use tact. While you should never say anything like, "No you can't search my bag. You got a warrant?" instead say, "Officer, I'd really rather you didn't. There are embarrassing photos of me and my girlfriend in there, and she'd kill me if she knew I let you see them." And if the officer is suspect of you hiding something, offer, "If you had a warrant I'd let you. At least *that* way I could tell her I had no choice."

So stand your ground, but be tactful about it. Remember the saying *you get more flies with honey than with vinegar*? Well it should stand here, too. Keep in mind the fact that they will lie to get you into trouble, *just* because you were rude to them. Just make sure they know you are not afraid of them because you are aware of your rights.

Step 3. Shut the F*** Up: In the event of your arrest, remember your Fifth Amendment right. In case you have either forgotten, or are unaware of your right, it is as follows:

"No person shall be held to answer for a capital, or otherwise infamous crime,

Unless on a presentment or indictment of a Grand Jury, except in cases arising

In the land or naval forces, or in the Militia, when in actual service in time of

War or public danger; nor shall any person be subject for the same offense tw-

ice put in jeopardy of life or limb; nor shall be compelled in any criminal case to

be a witness against himself, nor be deprived of life, liberty, or property, with-

out due process of law; nor shall private property be taken for public use, with-

out just compensation."

-The Constitution of

The United States of America

Amendment V

Yes, that is correct. You have the right to NOT incriminate yourself. The best way to not incriminate is to remain silent. They even tell you that you have the right to remain silent when you get arrested!

Far too many people get busted because they talked. Thankfully, our Founding Fathers were crooks too, and left us a little loophole to help ourselves out of a jamb. I recommend reading the Constitution of the United States of America, because there are a lot of other rights as well that can help you to beat cases.

Step 4. Bribe When Necessary: Sometimes you just won't be able to deny anything. At this point, what have you got to lose? Try bribing someone like a juror, a judge, or even the officer when he first arrests you.

You know you are going to jail, and there is only one other option (which we will discuss in step 5) other than bribing. Try your hand at it. Who knows, maybe you will have a continued working relationship with that person you bribed, and they may be eager to earn more in the future. If you can cultivate a relationship with that person, you can pull favors in the future. Like having the police arrest your enemies and plant evidence, for example.

When bribery fails, there is one more thing you can do...

Step 5. Eliminate the Opposition: Sometimes, people will not be able to take a hint. If you are detained, you would not like any witness to testify. Although eyewitness testimonies can account for a majority of convictions in the past, today it isn't as effective.

According to research, "The power of suggestion is central in Perry v. New Hampshire, the U.S. Supreme Court case for which APA filed a brief on Aug. 5. Perry addresses whether courts, in affording a defendant due process, must review the validity of all eyewitness testimony that was obtained with improperly suggestive tactics. New Hampshire requires such a review only if police or other state officials use improper tactics to obtain eyewitness identification, but not if suggestive tactics occur through happenstance. In Perry, a witness, unsolicited by police, identified the defendant after seeing him through her window standing with the police who were detaining him in handcuffs. Later, the witness was unable to describe him or pick him out of a photo lineup. Still, because the police did not sway her early identification, the court allowed it into evidence."(Azar, 2011).

Not only can witnesses succumb to the power of suggestion, but they rely on what *their* perception is, and what *their* memory of the event was. Human memory cannot be reliable as it is all too clouded. Remember the "fog of war" and confusing the witnesses discussed in the chapter on robbery? This will be of help. But just in case you don't put enough fear into someone, to make them know better than to rat you out, you *will* need to kill them. Yes; *you may have to commit murder.*

You will not be able to do it yourself, so you have to have someone else do it. Either have a friend do it, or hire a professional. It makes no difference in the outcome.

If there are no witnesses, you may have to kill the arresting officers. This will result in mistrial in most US counties. If the officers are dead, they will not be able to testify in court, and will not be able to account for any illegal doings. Keep in mind, however, this won't work with the FBI. If they arrest you, you may just have to bite the bullet. Maybe literally, it's up to you.

In some cases, you can threaten the jurors, and get them to understand how innocent you are. If they don't want to comply, kill one of them, or a relative of one of them if you're feeling particularly diabolical. They will get the picture rather quickly.

In review:

Step 1. Be Cordial

The bigger the douchebag, the tighter the cuffs.

Step 2. Don't Resist, but be Stern

Seriously, check out nevergetbusted.com.

Step 3. Shut the F* Up**

Just say you plead da fif

Step 4. Bribe When Necessary

Everyone has a price. Find it.

Step 5. Eliminate the Opposition

Dead men tell no tales.

Epilogue

In a world where the stressors on money are becoming increasingly apparent, and the ideal of the American Dream is looking more and more disillusioned, all men are forced to do what they must in order to provide. While the judge is feared for his sentencing, know that no man could ever truly judge another. Fear not what others do, be brave, and be a frontiersman of the land you give yourself.

To tow a fine line is to handicap yourself. You are destined for better things, and you owe it to yourself to achieve those things. If other people are profiting from your loss, then it must be time for you to return the favor. Fear not the future. While you may not see what lies ahead, understand there is no need to fear it. When a car travels at night, does its driver see the entire stretch of road or just what the headlights allow? When you climb a stair case, you must do it step by step.

There is no such thing as an honest person, truly 100% honest. Know this, and you will know how to succeed.

Disclaimer: The information within this book is strictly

intended for entertainment purposes. In no way does the author, publishing house, or any affiliate thereof condone or encourage the use of this information in any way that is against the law. Do not attempt any of the things found inside, and if you choose to do so, you are 100% liable for the subsequent repercussions.

Furthermore, its purpose is to show the blatant criminal tactics that are used in everyday business; including big name corporations, and the government.

References

BJS, Federal Justice Statistics 2006, Statistical Tables, NCJ 225711, May 2009.

Frederick Hegney v. Carlyle I. Holder, U. S. Court of Appeals for the 11th Circuit (April 21, 2006)

Cook, W. A. (2008). King of the bootleggers: a biography of George Remus. : McFarland and Co.

www.cga.ct.gov

http://www.armstronglegal.com.au/criminal-law/offences/stealing/receiving-stolen-goods

http://www.fbi.gov/chicago/press-releases/2014/former-cook-county-official-sentenced-to-51-months-in-prison-for-steering-contracts-in-return-for-nearly-35-000-in-kickbacks

http://www.pagepate.com/experience/criminal-defense/federal-crimes/federal-money-laundering/

Azar, B. (2011). The limits of eyewitness testimony: APA.org December 2011, Vol 42, No. 11

Made in the USA
Middletown, DE
17 October 2018